Pacific Island Scrapbook

Written and photographed by Angie and Andy Belcher

Contents

Collins

Vanuatu – the country

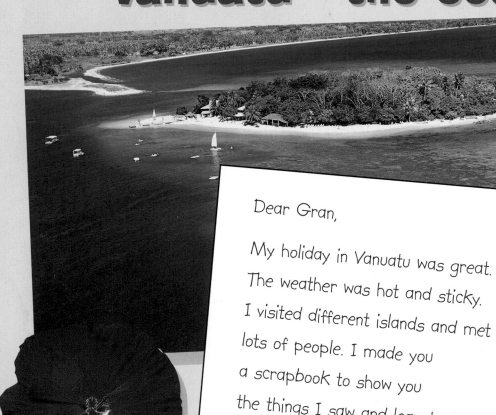

Dear Gran,

My holiday in Vanuatu was great.
The weather was hot and sticky.
I visited different islands and met
lots of people. I made you
a scrapbook to show you
the things I saw and learnt.

Love from Amy

Granny Jones
5, Park Rd
Weatherville
United Kingdom
UKI 3GB

Vanuatu has 83 islands which stretch over 1300 km.

The islands were formed millions of years ago when underwater volcanoes were pushed to the Earth's surface.

Some of the volcanoes are still active.

3

Coral reefs grow around many of the islands. The reefs are made by tiny animals that grow hard shells to protect them.

It takes millions and millions of these shells to build a reef.

Port Vila

Port Vila is the capital of Vanuatu. It's on Efate Island. There are lots of shops and cafés here. There's also a huge market that sells food, flowers and **souvenirs**.

You can buy hundreds of different types of shells there too.

Village life

Whole families live together in the villages. Many of them grow food in their gardens and catch fish from their canoes.

What they don't eat themselves,
they sell at the market.

sweet potatoes

bananas

coconuts

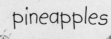

pineapples

yams

Rivers are important because people use them for drinking, swimming and washing.

My new friends told me stories while the washing dried on the warm stones.

I visited my new friends at school.

We walked on stilts ...

... and played volleyball on the beach.

A traditional village.

Some people choose to live the **traditional** way in villages that haven't changed for hundreds of years.

Their houses are made from **palm** leaves. The children learn to weave, carve, dance, play the **pan flute** and look after the gardens.

Me, holding a pan flute.

This girl is holding a carved pole.

This old man is weaving some rope.

A boy washing clothes.

Festivals

Festivals celebrate special events.

On Pentecost Island people celebrate a good yam harvest by land diving. Land diving is like bungee jumping.

Was this the first bungee jump?

Each year on Ambrym Island the Rom Dance takes place. The dancers dress up in banana-leaf costumes and wear huge masks.

The masks are amazing!

13

On Tanna Island
the villagers celebrate
boys becoming men and
girls becoming women.

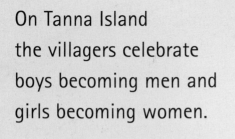

Everyone dresses up.

The villagers
painted my face.

We danced all night.

Language

More than 105 different languages are spoken in Vanuatu.
Bislama is the language everyone can speak.

English	Bislama
Good morning	Gudmoning
Goodnight	Gudnaet
Goodbye	Tata
How are you?	Yu orate?
What is your name?	Wanem blong yu?
My name is ...	Nem blong me ...

I learnt some words in Bislama.

17

Animals

Lots of animals live on the islands.
Flying foxes are really bats. They live in
the trees and are good to eat.

Pigs are a sign of **wealth**.
They are eaten on special occasions.

Some people keep parrots as pets.

Plants

Our bush guide showed us plants that can cure colds, poison fish and make bows and arrows for hunting.

These plants are really useful!

Some plants have many uses, like coconuts. You can:

drink the milk,

burn the **husk** for firewood,

weave the leaves from the tree,

eat the flesh,

carve the shell.

Where in the world is Vanuatu?

North America

Europe

Asia

Africa

South America

Australia

New Zealand

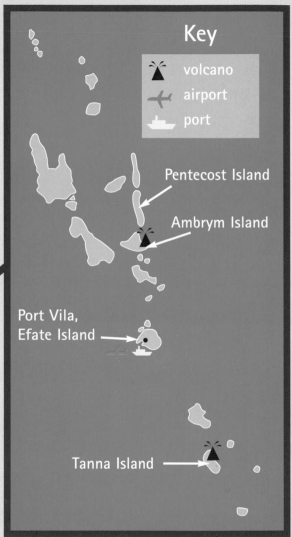

Key

☀ volcano

✈ airport

⚓ port

Pentecost Island

Ambrym Island

Port Vila,
Efate Island

Tanna Island

Glossary

Bislama – the main language of Vanuatu

husk – the outer part of the coconut that isn't eaten

palm – a tree with large leaves found in hot countries

pan flute – a musical instrument

souvenirs – things that are kept as reminders of a person, place or event

traditional – a way of doing things that has gone on for a very long time

wealth – riches

:paw: Ideas for reading :paw:

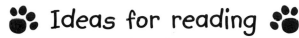

Written by Kelley Taylor
Educational Consultant

Learning objectives: Use the terms fiction and non-fiction, noting differing features; identify simple questions and use text to find answers; locate parts of text that give particular information; know that glossaries give definitions and explanations and know what definitions are; in a group, listen to each other's views and preferences, agree the next steps and identify each member's contributions.

Curriculum links: Geography: An island home; Where in the world is Barnaby Bear?

Interest words: Vanuatu, Bislama, husk, palm, pan flute, souvenirs, traditional, wealth

Resources: world map or globe

Word count: 589

Getting started

- Using a world map or globe, ask the children to locate their own country. Explain that today's book is a scrapbook of Amy's trip to a Pacific island, Vanuatu (Vah-noo-ah-too). Can the children find it on the map/globe?

- Ask the children to discuss what they would like to find out about life in Vanuatu, e.g. *Do the people speak English?*

- Read the back cover together and ensure that all the children try pronouncing Vanuatu. Model formulating a question about Vanuatu, and ask the children each to make a question themselves.

- Before reading on, ask: *Is this book fiction or non-fiction? Why?*

Reading and responding

- Ask the children to read the chapter headings on the contents page. *Will we find answers to any of our questions in this book?*

- Explain that, because this is a non-fiction text, they do not have to read it from the beginning – e.g *Because your question is about language you're*